Waterfalls

Nova Scotia's Masterpieces

Donna Barnett
with text by Allan Billard

NIMBUS
PUBLISHING

Nimbus Publishing Limited

PO Box 9166

Halifax, NS B3K 5M8

(902) 455-4286

Design: Margaret Issenman, MGDC

Donna Barnett photo: Anne Wonham

Allan Billard photo: Donna Barnett

Library and Archives Canada Cataloguing in Publication

Billard, Allan, 1949-

Waterfalls : Nova Scotia's masterpieces / text by Allan Billard ;

photography by Donna Barnett.

ISBN 13: 978-1-55109-612-4   ISBN 10: 1-55109-612-9

1. Waterfalls—Nova Scotia—Guidebooks. 2. Trails—Nova Scotia—Guidebooks.
3. Nova Scotia—Guidebooks. I. Barnett, Donna II. Title.

GV199.44.C2B54 2007   796.51'09716   C2007-900095-9

We acknowledge the financial support of the Government of Canada through the Book Publishing Industry Development Program (BPIDP) and the Canada Council, and of the Province of Nova Scotia through the Department of Tourism, Culture and Heritage for our publishing activities.

Acknowledgements

The exact locations of many waterfall sites in Nova Scotia are not widely known. Even with good directions, it is often difficult to find some sites without a local guide. We were always very fortunate in that regard. People we spoke with were more than willing to share their knowledge of the hard-to-get-to places and we appreciate all the thoughtful directions and safety tips.

It is encouraging to see how several waterfall sites are being developed by local authorities in an environmentally friendly way, so that the people who come to these falls tomorrow can be as rewarded by their natural beauty as we are today.

Some, like regional biologist Doug Archibald, were very eager to lead us to little-known waterfalls and to relate stories of how fish and wildlife play their roles in these unique mini-ecosystems. Others, including Kim and Bev Williams, were willing to point out the best routes to take into the steep gorges and to share the beauty of their land with us.

Finally, Allen, Emma, and Alexander Chapman were always eager to join us as we trekked into unknown territory, seeking out yet another storied waterfall site. It wouldn't have been nearly as much fun doing this book without them.

Donna Barnett and Allan Billard

Contents

Introduction

The first peoples in Nova Scotia to make a strong connection between waterfall sites and peace of mind were likely the native Mi'kmaq. As with any hunter-gatherer society, it can be assumed that the Mi'kmaq made good use of waterfalls. Fish often congregate at the base of falls to rest before their ascent, and other wildlife, especially the "young-of-the-year," sometimes tumble to their death from a waterfall precipice. Both these scenarios make for good food gathering. There are at least three places in Nova Scotia called "Indian Falls," but no legend or reference of their activities there has survived into modern-day writings.

It was common in colonial times to choose a place name based on the most prominent feature at that location. In this province, no one feature seems more prominent in a site's naming than its connection to water, and often, to a waterfall.

There are several predictable place names like Fall River, Fall Lake, Falls Bog, Big Falls, and Fall Brook. The province is also home to many unique names, like Apron Falls, Bad Falls, Buggy Hole Falls, Burned Potato Falls and, of course, Bangs Falls; it is impossible to review the whole list!

It was as a practical resource that waterfalls were first sought out by European settlers in this new land. Waterfalls provided indispensable power for sawmills and gristmills and, as the communities grew, for carding mills.

Waterfalls also helped in one very unique development for Nova Scotia in the early 1800s: the establishment of overland marine railways, consisting of cradles placed on tracks that ran up an incline between two bodies of water. Ships of the day would sail into the cradle and wait for the power generated by water flowing down into a turbine, which would then wind the cables and haul the ship up the slope. The vessel could then slide off the cradle and into the next part of the river or lake. There were two of these marine railways on the Shubenacadie Canal, for example, each powered by the water flowing from one lake to another.

Later, the more entrepreneurial of the new settlers devised ways to produce electricity from waterfalls. A height difference of only a few feet was enough to create a current. It was

Dawson Brook Falls

The Dawson Brook waterfall appears as it must have before Europeans came to these woodlands. The faint trail into the top of the gorge is overshadowed by old hemlock and pine, and the forest floor is soft with deep layers of last year's foliage. The rays of the sun rarely break through the canopy, discouraging all but a few bunchberry and hearty blueberry plants. Huge tracts of this landscape are still under the control of longtime owners, the Joudrey family. They have cut and sold wood for generations here, although they now deal more in recycled wood fibre than in newly cut product. Even though the valuable stands of timber on the surrounding hills have largely been cut, Joudrey's loggers bypassed many acres of commercial softwood at this jagged gorge. The family is familiar with this site and is proud of how it stands as at least a small reminder of the respect that needs to be given to the environment.

The faint trail to the falls seems to disappear at about the same time the gorge becomes visible. There is a choice of good perches that offer a view right into the chasm, but no access down to the base of the falls.

Dawson Brook has its headwaters just upstream from the falls, the only stream that drains a marsh called Stillwater Station. There is rarely enough water to ensure the falls a year-round supply, however. When there is good water volume, Dawson Brook flows full for a few hundred metres and then splashes water everywhere as it drops over a precipitous six-storey lip into the gorge below. At these times, the site is dramatic. During a long, dry summer, the gorge sits almost empty. Whatever the water conditions, the site is a sanctuary from the whir and rush of humanity. Even though a four-lane, high-speed highway passes just a few hundred metres to the east, the waterfall gorge on Dawson Brook is a reminder that life sometimes can stand still.

Indian Falls

LaHave River

Anglers come to Indian Falls on the north branch of the LaHave River because it is one of those places where the fish gather and rest during their long journey upstream to spawn. They also come here for the same reason hundreds of other visitors do—to enjoy the open and airy site, and to gaze upon a magnificent waterfall.

As in all river systems, the spring rains really swell the LaHave. The broad, grey cliff that faces the afternoon sun becomes completely awash at this time of year and the falls project a powerful presence. It is a marvel that fish could ever navigate up the torrent of water. Late in the summer, there is much less water volume and the falls are much less impressive than how they appeared just a few months earlier.

The Lunenburg District Municipality, recognizing the site's value as a tourist attraction, has built a new access road. They even carved out a large parking lot near the site. As word spreads that these formerly private lands are now easy to access, the area near the falls will become a favourite family destination. It is large enough for all to enjoy the grassy fields, the colourful wildflowers, and the many species of migratory birds that are also attracted to waterfalls.

While all waterfall sites present a danger to hikers, particularly small children who always seem to head straight for the edge of any cliff, the lands around Indian Falls are fairly safely to wander. A rough ten-metre descent to the base of the cliff offers access to a very pleasant gravel beach used by fly fishermen, and even better views of the site than from above.

Mill Falls

Mill Falls is a big noisy site that any music composer would draw inspriation from. The rapids where the Mersey River flows freely over several rocky ledges, then into one larger drop to the rocks below, creates a chocolate-coloured mass of brown water and white bubbles.

The most attractive characteristic of the Mersey is certainly its colour. Indeed, all the colours at this Kejimkujik National Park site are fantastic. A great variety of plant life combines with the white foam and the green reflections on the brown water to display quite vividly what makes this a jewel in Canada's national park system.

The short path from the parking area quickly meets the rushing water and follows the length of the falls. People seem drawn to their own favourite sections, whether it is the upper rapids, behind the fence next to the actual falls, or right out on the rocks at the bottom, inches away from the frothing water. With safe access to the water, this can be an "up-close-and-personal" falls, plus the site has everything needed for family nature outings like washrooms, well-maintained pathways, picnic tables, and a covered patio with wood stoves.

Indian Falls

Meteghan River

The receding glaciers carved out a fairly quiet channel for the Meteghan River, but just before the river reaches the salt waters of St. Mary's Bay, it drops almost two storeys in a triumphant crash. It is at that point that a dramatic fault line split the earth's crust over five hundred million years ago.

The broad white falls can easily be seen from the old highway bridge at St. Benoni, just fifty kilometres north of Yarmouth. Draining a very small part of the region, one would expect that the river would be almost dry in the summer and fall, but the source for this river is a group of three lakes and the falls are almost always full of water. There is a long, straight stretch of river at the point of the falls and on a sunny afternoon the site always presents a sparkling display.

Indian Falls does not attract very much attention, though, perhaps because the back road to reach it is seldom travelled, and few people know what a lovely tableau the falls make, even when viewed through the car window. There is little access directly up to the falls and that may discourage casual visitors who would like to become more familiar with the site. It is like a gem in a museum display: in full view, but just out of grasp.

Lake Brook Falls

Digby Neck is blessed with an unusually grand number of unique natural features. Many thousands of ecotourists arrive each year to see the Balancing Rock and towering basalt cliffs, the raised bogs with their unique plant and animal species, and of course, the whales. There are more whales and more species of marine mammals along these rocky shores than anywhere else in North America. It is ironic that as many people as there are who come to see the vibrant natural history of the area, few visitors ever even hear of the lovely falls on Lake Brook.

Just outside the busy fishing village of Sandy Cove, this obscure site remains much as it has since the fault first opened up, some two hundred million years ago. The falls are not marked by a trailhead sign or identified on any map. The stream flows only a short distance from its source, Lake Midway, before it drops directly over a twenty-five-metre cliff, emptying into Lake Brook Cove and St. Mary's Bay—a short but dramatic journey. It is one of the few waterfalls in western Nova Scotia, but perhaps it is just as well that people do not visit the site. There is really no place to capture the full view of the waterfall except from the base, which can only be accessed by climbing down into the loose rock gorge right beside the falls. Once at the bottom of the cliff, there is no place to stand.

Delaps Cove Falls

Like so many other sites, the falls at Delaps Cove are well away from the main highway and a long way down an old logging road. The Annapolis County Recreation Department has developed a well-groomed walking trail into the falls, though, and encourages visitors to make the effort to enjoy this site on the picturesque North Mountain.

The 1.8-kilometre loop trail starts at a parking lot just a few kilometres past Parkers Cove. There are clean pit toilets and informative pamphlets for new visitors. While the waterfall is its primary attraction, the trail is also designed to offer a full view of the Bay of Fundy as well as some of the wooded farmlands that attracted United Empire Loyalists and ex-slaves more than two hundred years ago. The unbelievably rocky landscape gives an idea of why their settlements have long been abandoned. The fishing industry has prospered along this shore, but farming must never have advanced past subsistence level.

Upon arriving at the waterfall, however, all thoughts of pioneer hardship disappear. The water of Bohaker Brook splashes off dozens of ancient basalt ledges in a classic veil-like display, falling fifteen metres into the Bay of Fundy. Flotsam and jetsam litter the cove below as the huge tides wash in long-dead trees and float them out again. When the tide is out, there is a gravel bar which looks great for beachcombing, but there is no way down to it other than descending the rocky cliff.

The site presents a visitor-friendly image. Being open to the Bay of Fundy, it is bright and airy, yet still wild and unspoiled. The trail is level and will present no difficulty for most. While there is a small viewing platform at the top of the falls, there are also several safe places to sit and share a picnic lunch in full view of the falls. The falls can also be comfortably enjoyed from a grassy ledge on the opposite side of the cove, and as a result, people often stay a little longer here than at other waterfall sites, waiting to watch the first signs of sunset before they reluctantly return to civilization.

Baxters Harbour Falls

The ocean can be harsh and unforgiving, but can also be captivating and picturesque. Baxters Harbour is a small fishing community on the Bay of Fundy shore that offers proof of both of these aspects of life beside the Atlantic.

Like many fishing villages, there are only two principal roads; one connects all the homes and the other leads to the wharf. Both roads in this community offer pleasant views, but it's the wharf road that ends at the water's edge that offers a real seaside experience. This is an active harbour, particularly during the lobster season when the boats challenge the mighty Bay of Fundy daily and wrest enough of a livelihood in the good weather to survive the bad.

The harbour also proudly boasts a waterfall, one that can be comfortably enjoyed right from the front seat of a car. Follow the wharf road down to the stony beach, take in the classic Maritime scenery, then simply turn to face the way you came. If the stream is full and the tide is high, the falls will be splashing right into the sea. If the tide is low, the cascade will crash upon the beach, disappearing into the seaweed.

The falls are not high and not always full. Careful examination will reveal that when the main road in the village was carved along the edge of the seawall, the highway engineers dug a drainage trough for the stream and enclosed it in a culvert that passes under the road. This actually hides the stream just above the falls before it re-emerges at the top of the cliff. It all sounds like a very industrial way to treat a natural stream, but having a waterfall drop straight into a quaint fishing harbour—in front of rustic fishing shacks and right beside several dories at their moorings—makes a perfect postcard tableau.

Working in the fishery is not an easy way to make a living, especially on the Bay of Fundy, but arriving back in Baxters Harbour after a long morning at sea and catching a glimpse of that special cascade is at least a small reward.

Moores Falls

Sometimes Nova Scotia hides its waterfalls deep in the wilderness. At other times, the enchantment of a pretty waterfall site is right next to a major highway. Just on the outskirts of Kentville, Highway 101 passes through North Alton and crosses Moores Brook. It is here that the brook chooses to descend several metres in a rush that obligingly faces the highway.

A broad rock outcrop spreads the gentle brook out like a blanket, almost as wide as the falls are high. People stop at this busy highway's edge to take in the view for a few minutes because the sound of the falling water and the comforting image of a wall of water sliding down the rock face present such a nice alternative to the rushing of the traffic.

It is not a major waterfall bowl by any measure. There is no torrent of water, no dark

and mysterious pool at its base. Moores Falls is simply one of nature's wilderness tableaus. It stands as an example of how cascading water can hold a person's gaze and capture the human spirit, even with the rush of traffic just a few steps away.

Millet Falls

For most of the year, the small stream supplying Millet Falls lightly trips over the rocks and makes one small drop into Falls Lake, near the highway between Chester and Windsor. It is an extremely peaceful spot where the woods are quietly dappled in sunlight. But in spring, a torrent of white, raging water fills the falls with a crashing heard throughout the woods, the stream being driven through the small chute of rocks. There is actually little elevation change and most of the river is accessible. It is a pretty spot, but not really a picnic site. There is little access to the stream, few places to sit and oftentimes, an insufferable hoard of blackflies.

Falls Lake does not get its name from these falls. Rather, a falls at the other end of the lake was one of the first hydro-generation sites in the province. That site is dry, however, having had its water supply completely diverted into a flume for the power turbine.

Sleepy Cove Falls

Two centuries ago, pioneer settlements dotted the landscape near Sleepy Cove. Transportation in and out was possible either along the cart paths or by small barges that plied the Shubenacadie Canal carrying lumber, bricks, and other goods to and from Halifax. Until recently, there wasn't even a trail into the falls at Sleepy Cove, just a short road into the western side of Grand Lake. The only way to access the wilderness site was by canoe. Each summer, several small parties of picnickers would make the trip up from their cottage on Grand Lake or over from Laurie Provincial Park on the eastern shoreline. They were the fortunate few who got to enjoy the natural peace of this isolated site.

Now the abandoned farms are being taken over by modern homes. King Brook, which

quietly drained Haunted Lake and Henry Meadow for thousands of years, now shares its surroundings with an encroaching suburb. The road that leads to the new homes is almost up to the brook and its small falls, known as Sleepy Cove Falls. It is such a natural site that many hope that the encroaching suburbia will be carefully harmonized with the site's natural beauty, the one complementing the other.

Sleepy Cove Falls lies only a few metres upstream from the outfall of King Brook, separated into at least three sections as it bends around the grey quartzite rock outcrop. The rocks are easy and fun to scale, even for small children, and they may be covered in blueberry or raspberry bushes, adding to the day's delight. This is a very bright waterfall site that is not shrouded in a deep gorge but open to the midday sun and airy breezes that waft in from the large lake. This, plus the fact that Sleepy Cove offers a natural windbreak, makes the area a favourite stop on a sailing cruise, a place to nap after a morning of waterskiing or windsurfing.

St. Croix Falls

In the 1920s, there were many entrepreneurs eager to set up industries in Nova Scotia, but there was no electricity outside of a few main towns. Some of these business people owned vast tracts of rural land and realized that they might be able to harness their own rivers for hydroelectric power. They correctly determined that water does not need to drop from vast heights to turn wheels and gears that generate electric current. After all, the waters of the province had given the early settlers the power they needed for sawmills, for grinding their grain, and for carding their flax, so this new idea for water power seemed to meet the new wave of industrialization.

One of the province's first successful water power developments was in St. Croix, near Windsor. There, the stream that drained Panuke Lake dropped from enough of a height that it held good potential for power generation.

When it was dammed and the Panuke Lake reservoir expanded to its present length of over twenty-five kilometres, the supply of power for this part of rural Nova Scotia was assured. Many more streams were harnessed in this way and the rural areas were electrified.

As Nova Scotia joined the new industrial age, it lost many very pretty waterfall sites, however. St. Croix Falls, for example, had most—but not all—of its water channelled through a large pipe into the turbine. The old powerhouse does seem to blend into the landscape, though, and the watery cascade outside still offers a restful stop along the old Highway 1 to Windsor. It seems to explain the important bounty nature can provide, while reminding us of the value of the remaining waterfall sites.

Butchers Falls

Three of Nova Scotia's best-known rivers have their beginnings in the same uplands. The headwaters of the Musquodoboit, the St. Mary's, and the Stewiacke Rivers all mingle at much the same area where the lines of Guysborough, Halifax, Colchester, and Cumberland counties intersect. Each of the rivers carves its way down to the sea, following ancient valleys in some locations and creating new pathways in others. The Stewiacke River watershed includes several accessible waterfall sites.

Goshen Brook makes a short trip from blueberry fields at the top of Butcher Hill to the Stewiacke River. Its most attractive characteristic is the fifteen-metre waterfall—known as Butchers Fall—located halfway between the rural hamlets of Upper Musquodoboit and Upper Stewiacke, which is located right where the brook runs beside the road connecting the two communities. The path into the base of the falls is short and level, but it is marked only by a small opening in the roadside foliage. As the seasons pass, the opening is less and less visible. The abandoned farmstead across from the path—the original home of the Butcher family—is also slowly being overwhelmed by nature.

As if in defiance of nature's attempts to reclaim these lands, the brook has chosen this spot to make a loud impression and to refuse to go gently into the peacefulness of the Stewiacke River. Fortunately, there are several rocky perches that offer a variety of perspectives, including one showing the full height of the falls. No shutterbug should come away from Butchers Falls without lasting images of how a very minor stream can suddenly become a showy cascade before returning again to a babbling woodland brook.

Upper Burnside Falls

The pleasant little waterfall at Upper Burnside is the centrepiece of a small park established by a few proud local residents. A small picnic site has been created as well, as part of the invitation to visitors to descend the many steps and enjoy the peace that these falls offer. The babbling of Meadow Brook at the base of the staircase seems to overtake all of our modern realities.

Appearing more like a gentle cascade than a waterfall, the brook tumbles over a series of ledges and into a broad, shallow pool. The placid, reflective surface invites visitors to doff their shoes and socks and wade into the cool water. The pool seems completely at peace for the longest time, gently lazing beside the fiddleheads and maple trees, before easing its way back up to a gentle flow to join the Pembroke River somewhere downstream. Shortly after, it becomes part of the Stewiacke River, taking the water from this pleasant oasis in Upper Burnside to the Bay of Fundy and the highest tides in the world—all in a matter of a few kilometres.

Fall Brook Falls

If there was to be a back-to-nature retreat in this province, the hinterland around Trafalgar in northern Nova Scotia would be the best place to establish it. There, in the backcountry where the Guysborough, Halifax, Pictou, and Colchester county lines intersect, the pioneer homesteads have been all but reclaimed, and many of the wood roads returned to deer trails. Nature itself seems to be in control again.

There is still an active forest industry here as new tracts of land are harvested, but the fresh greenery of a successive forest quickly moves into the clearings. Bears forage throughout this new growth, and it is common for eagles to soar overhead, searching for some fresh food to take back to the nest.

Fall Brook shares this spectacular scenery. Its waters run slowly for several kilometres through the thick new forest, then more quickly over rocky outcroppings before finally joining the Stewiacke River on its way to the Bay of Fundy.

Starting from Highway 289 near Sheepherders Junction, a rough path parallels the brook, following an ancient cart path up to the falls. Framed by aggressive softwood saplings, the water splays recklessly over a large hummock of rock. The falls do not fall, but rather spread out and run down the ten-metre-high rock face.

The falls on Falls Brook are one of nature's classrooms, a place where the elements of life interact. The combination of fresh running water, thick woody cover, and tender new plant shoots makes a perfect home for both prey and predator.

Victoria Park Falls

Truro is a very fortunate town. There are very few municipalities in Nova Scotia that can boast a four-hundred-hectare wilderness park right in the centre of the community. The popular Victoria Park straddles two ancient rock formations, one composed of grey sandstone estimated at 350 million years old, and the other made up of rocks some 10 million years younger. In the spring, when the waters of Lepper Brook are flowing freely, the park has another valuable asset: a pair of signature waterfalls.

A network of short hiking trails and steps leads through several rocky gorges, making it relatively easy for modern-day adventurers to access the falls. It wasn't the same for the one-time premier of Nova Scotia, Joe Howe. When he visited Truro in 1830, he had to struggle over the cliffs and along the stream bed itself just to visit the falls. Still, he returned from his adventure extremely impressed with the site and wrote about the pleasant journey. Years later, the lower falls were named in his honour.

The upper cascade is Waddell Falls, for Susan Waddell Stevens, who also appreciated the natural beauty of the lands owned by her family. Victoria Park was created from her bequest of the original land in 1888. She felt that the land should always remain open to the residents of Truro and for visitors who might like to enjoy the unique geological formations that continue to be eroded by the brook. Over the years, the town has added to the park and made great improvements to the trails.

Although the falls are most spectacular in spring, the park, with its two waterfalls and sturdy viewing platforms, remains a pleasant wilderness retreat at any time, well worth the visit.

Annandale Falls

Many of the waterfalls in Nova Scotia were created long ago when the surface layers of the earth shifted. The resulting gorges are narrow, steep, and extremely difficult to access. Other waterfalls resulted less dramatically when the rivers draining high plateaus simply carved their way through the earth's exterior all the way to the seacoast. However they were formed, there are some waterfalls in Nova Scotia that are just too difficult to approach safely.

The falls just northeast of the Wentworth Valley are one such example—a site that no one, not even experienced rock climbers, can take for granted. The walls of the gorge next to the waterfall are thirty-five metres high and extremely steep where the east branch of Swan Brook comes roaring out of the Cobequid mountain range. Complicating the descent into this secluded canyon is the very loose terrain and the lack of anything substantial to hold on to.

All that having been stated—and putting the return ascent out of mind—once down at the base of the falls the misty aura is captivating. It is overwhelming to be next to a giant veil of whitewater that tumbles ceaselessly out of the solid grey rock face. The flush of water seems to fly down the ten-metre drop before, almost in an instant, it becomes just another rocky brook, at peace with its surroundings and ready to move along.

In spite of the uneven landscape, a thick undergrowth and mixed hardwood overstorey make up most of the vegetation in the gorge. Wildflowers almost carpet the forest floor, bringing many butterflies and other insects to the margins of the babbling stream. It is a perfect lesson in the amazing variety which nature provides.

Wentworth Valley Falls

One of the best-kept secrets in Nova Scotia is this intimate waterfall site. Like several other hidden waterfalls, it can be accessed by anyone with a desire to discover a simple natural pleasure. But like the other falls in the well-known Wentworth Valley, most remain largely ignored.

When the Trans-Canada Highway used to pass through this popular skiing destination prior to 1997, upwards of ten thousand people a day would drive right past this lovely cascade, completely unaware that it was just a few metres off the west side of the road, behind a grove of spruce trees. The access road is unmarked, except for a simple iron post a few hundred metres south of the Wentworth Motel. The track is rough and rutted, but the walk is short and the reward great.

This is one of the true "bridal veil" falls in the province. When it is full of water there are few falls anywhere that offer a more postcard-perfect image. There is no deep gorge, no broad bowl, not even a deep, dark pool at the base, just a solid wall of whitewater spreading latterly from the apex. Unfortunately, the natural supply of water feeding these falls is only a small watershed atop a few local hills. Without a constant supply of water there is no guarantee that the flow will cover the wide rock face. There is always at least some water

running here, however, and the wading pool at the base of the falls offers another simple pleasure—a perfect place for the kids to splash in the water.

On some bright morning following a few days of rain, take the "old" highway through the Wentworth Valley and stop for a lunch at this special place. Let the rest of the world speed by as you enjoy the sun shining down onto the picnic area.

Londonderry Falls

Travelling down the old road into Londonderry is like stepping through a portal, back into the 1880s. The main street still sports the general store, a union hall, and some of the railway works of its iron ore glory days. When Acadia Mines fueled the local economy, five thousand people worked here and a number of their homes still remain—a testament to the craftsmanship of those hard days. It was, in fact, Nova Scotia's original boomtown.

That was the past, however. Today, Londonderry focuses upon more enduring assets, including the tourism potential of several waterfalls. Both the Great Village River and Rockland Brook plunge happily along for kilometres in their separate canyons and then meet just beyond the town centre. They both offer a number of waterfall gorges, but only a few are accessible.

The town has remedied this to some extent by creating a parking lot and small picnic area near the top of a particularly dramatic gorge on Great Village River. It is fenced for a very good reason, as the drop into the chasm could be disastrous. The site is really best seen from above anyway, as these falls seem to be more of a rapid succession of sharp drops around unending twists and turns than a typical waterfall with distinct top and base.

From the look-off, it is possible to watch the sparkling water thirty metres below as it crashes over many of these ledges of rock from the Londonderry formation, named for its iron carrying ores like limonite, hematite, and siderite. That image is softened, though, by the

 waving of the fern fronds clinging to their tiny footholds up and down the canyon walls.

Economy Falls

Economy Falls is the picturesque Nova Scotia waterfall that has been enjoyed by more people than the province's other sites. Young couples even come here to be married at the base of the canyon, the water providing a gorgeous background for their wedding photos.

Economy Falls was known for years as a pretty waterfall at the end of a fairly easy trail. Family groups regularly made the trek into the gorge, climbed all over the rocks and picnicked at the base, enjoying the bright airy scene. There is but one problem: a very long staircase which has so many steps that even going down into the gorge is tiring. The climb back up is aided a bit by a few benches placed partway up the ascent.

But a few years ago, the earth's crust shuddered without warning and the tons of rock that formed the lip at the top of the gorge cracked off and dropped ten metres. It created a mound of rubble in the middle of the cascade, forcing the water underneath and out of sight. Longtime hikers were aghast: tourism officials feared the worst. National radio programs even featured news reports about the sad loss of a provincial icon.

The outcome from the incident was not all that dramatic, however. The falls are still very pretty, with the river's flow continuing to gush out of the cliff about halfway down its full height. The water has realigned its course around the rubble, giving the new view a slightly bent appearance, but taking little away from the overall image. In the end, the mini-earthquake served as a reminder that the planet is still changing and that what we enjoy today is just a snapshot in time.

Hundreds of visitors still make the trip to Economy Falls each summer, enjoying it as much as ever, and gaining a firsthand lesson in the earth's active geology. The road into the area from Highway 2 has been upgraded, a parking lot added, and the short trail is even better marked than before. Much of the watershed and two long wilderness trails are now protected within the Economy River Wilderness Area. Protected from human beings, that is, but not from the power of nature.

North River Falls
Cobequid Range

Like many waterfall sites in Nova Scotia, this one is located on private land. Fortunately, however, this landowner does not prevent the public from enjoying it, as long as visitors are extremely careful. There is even a knotted rope strung between the trees over the loose rock gorge, showing the steep path down and helping with the climb back up.

All the river gorges in the Cobequid Hills seem to be made up of this loose rock and access is always very dangerous. It is only from the base, however, that the splendour of the site can be enjoyed.

When full of water, North River Falls presents an absolutely classic tableau. The river

drops over a grey rock face, crashing into a deep cold pool below. The gorge is over ten storeys deep, although the waterfall is not that high. A wide, grey bowl surrounds the waterfall, and is spotted with hardwood trees clinging to the ledges. There are even a few sentinel-like spruce trees perched right on the peak of the falls.

There are usually trout in the pool, too. Local anglers tell stories of coming here in the spring, just as dawn breaks over the cliff walls, and filling their daily limit before the sun is fully over the horizon.

As pretty as it is in the spring and after a rainstorm, the flow does decrease to little more than a trickle when the August sun and winds dry up the blueberry bogs in the highlands.

Like most things in Nova Scotia, blueberries included, there is a season when they are best enjoyed, and other times when memories will have to do.

Harrington Falls

Many visitors come to the Parrsboro shore to search for dinosaur fossils or to walk on the sea floor at low tide. Not far from this shore, and well worth a stop, is Harrington Falls, one of very few waterfalls that adventurous individuals can actually walk behind. Visiting the site is not a good idea for the unprepared, and perhaps it should even be posted as "dangerous," given the rugged descent into the gorge, but walking inside a waterfall is a unique experience worth the effort.

Harrington Falls is situated at the confluence of the Harrington River and its major tributary, the West Branch. There is rarely a lot of water in the falls, as the West Branch only drains a small plateau, but it is really quite high, and the water falls spectacularly in a long slender plume. Of greater interest is the series of small ledges behind it, allowing hikers a rare view from within. Of course, wet feet will be the result of the trek across the main stream and around the waterfall pool to the back of the falls. There is just no way to stay dry, as water splashes everywhere. Perhaps that is actually an advantage of this site, though, as the cool water is refreshing on a warm summer day. The exceedingly difficult climb back up and out of the gorge will require all the energy that a sip or two from the stream provides.

Moose River Falls

Everything about the landscape along the old Highway 2 to Parrsboro reminds the traveller how large nature is. The view on the south side is of vast tidal flats, red cliffs, and a grey horizon where the Bay of Fundy stretches for kilometres. The Cobequid Mountains rise hundreds of metres on the other side, filling the view to the north with stands of sturdy timber and rocky hills that have been there for over three hundred million years.

It is this ancient hinterland that hides Moose River Falls. Actually, it hides many other waterfalls as well, but a few locals know the one on the West Branch of the Moose River because an old logging road passes fairly close to the site. The rest of the waterfalls are accessible only by trudging up the forbidding McCallum Gulch or the rocky stream bed of the East Branch of the Moose River.

Getting from the logging road to the waterfall presents an extremely high degree of difficulty. The trail is poorly marked and rarely travelled, so it quickly becomes lost in the forest litter. At the top of the eighty-metre gorge, there is even less evidence of a way down. Only by grasping at scrawny birch trees and the branches of stunted spruce can the loose footholds be trusted. The rock in the gorge is old but it is not the hard granite or basalt of newer ranges. It is shale, silt, and sandstone and shatters at the touch. The same geology that creates challenging conditions for hikers, however, makes fabulous waterfall scenery for photographers.

The river has etched its way deep into the rocks of the gorge, leaving the actual falls only

a twenty-metre drop to the gravel below. It is possible to walk up the stream right to the cascade. The view may be a wet one, but it is a treat. As an unrelenting rush of water pounds the loose rocks, it is easy to imagine how more and more of the gorge is eroded and flushed away with each passing season. The power of nature is no more obvious than at the base of a three-hundred-million-year-old waterfall.

Hidden Falls

The geology of the Cobequid Mountains is a treasure, offering dinosaur fossils from the Carboniferous period and giving evidence of how the continents drifted apart eons before that. Sometimes it is an undistinguished rift in the ancient topography that provides the attraction, a place where the age of the rocks can be felt and smelled; Hidden Falls is such an attraction.

This is a narrow and dark site, shadowed by stands of mixed softwood that enjoy a microclimate kept damper than usual by the falling water. The cascade itself is divided into three sections, winding around the rock face and making it hard to view. Hidden Falls was the first waterfall along the Fundy shore to be opened for public viewing. The landowner carved out a trail behind his old farmhouse and erected a viewing platform at the point from which the three separated sections of the falls are best viewed. He also established a small gift shop and stocked it with the polished stones and semi-precious gems that appealed to the rockhounds who passed by.

The homestead is gone now and the site is gradually feeling the slow, eternal pressure to return to a natural state. There is no trace of the former buildings, with only a paragliding park and a windsock marking where the gift shop used to be. It all makes the name of the site prophetic.

The path to the site is easy to locate and it is quite passable. The falls are now enjoyed without the elevated view from the platform, making it impossible to see all three sections in one glance without getting a boost from a friend or climbing a tree.

Ripley Falls

Sometimes waterfalls are so far back into Nova Scotia's hinterland that the journey into them is too arduous for all but the determined hiker. This is because most waterfall sites are naturally associated with rugged land where ancient geological fault zones have broken up the terrain so much that it is almost impassable. On the other hand, sometimes waterfalls can be right in your own backyard. The stately Ripley home has one of the latter. Standing for more than one hundred years on a hillside in Lakelands, just a few kilometres north of Parrsboro, the home has a thirty-metre waterfall just minutes from its backdoor.

Actually, the home sits precisely on the Cobequid Fault. 320 million years ago, the earth shifted and the rock fractured, leaving huge cliffs over which tumble the many waterways that

drain the highlands. Jeffers Brook is one such stream. It flows for ten kilometres on its journey out of Cranberry Lake and the Gilbert Hills and down into the Bay of Fundy. Nowhere on that long and rugged descent does it drop with a more abrupt elegance than it does at Ripley Falls, where it splashes into an attractive pool surrounded by a classic sandstone bowl.

Wards Falls

Land grants by early governments and officials have resulted in most of the wilderness in Nova Scotia actually being owned by private citizens and local companies. Fortunately, many of Nova Scotia's landowners remain extremely public minded and encourage access to the scenic sites on their land. Such is the case with the timberland along the North Branch of the Diligent River, near Parrsboro, where a building supply company developed and still maintains the popular trail to Wards Falls.

A footpath follows the meandering river, crossing the clear running water in more than a dozen places and offering many pleasant rest stops to enjoy the flora and fauna. The trail rises sharply as it approaches the falls, however, and the lush vegetation gives way to large stony outcroppings. The gorge is typical of the entire Cobequid Fault scarp along this shore. The rivers etched their own paths through the rock, this one leaving a grotto-like cave at the top and Wards Falls to stand through the millennia. As with many of the tourist destinations in the Parrsboro area, it is this ancient hard rock geology that attracts most of the visitors.

While the falls are not very high, this site is attractive for another reason. A ladder has been erected up the cliff face on one side and risk-seekers can climb to the top, then lower themselves into position to peer into the cave. There is not too much to see, however, as the river seems to disappear into the rock and the cave is too small to explore.

Although many visitors come annually to share the wilderness experience, they leave it as natural as they found it—a fitting tribute to the private landowner who first developed this site.

Drysdale Falls

Drysdale Falls is a postcard waterfall, the site most people think of when Nova Scotia's waterfalls are mentioned. The water from Bailey's Brook drains the northern side of Nuttby Mountain, then falls in one single plunge over the fifteen-metre cliff directly into a dark pool. The falls are also enclosed within a semicircular amphitheatre, making them the most striking of the many small waterfalls that slice across the fault line through these uplands. The cliffs around the falls offer many good perches for photographers, and a steep but well-used trail leads to the large and sunlit beach below.

Sitting just off a well-known country road, Drysdale Falls is easy to get to. Because of its accessibility and its picturesque beauty, the site is almost always buzzing with visitors. There is far less plant cover and wildlife here than at other waterfalls, and the landowner worries about the added stress on the environment and the erosion of the trails. Fortunately, the falls themselves have been carved out of the enduring basalt formations that make up the backbone of the province. The site has withstood over 360 million years of geological

upheaval, so it will likely resist the wear and tear of the sightseers. Still, the thin soils on the forest floor bear the signs of heavy human traffic and the landowner is right to caution visitors about careless use of such a classic site.

Balmoral Mills

One of the most popular rest stops for tour buses along the Sunrise Trail is the old gristmill at Balmoral Mills. The structure is three storeys tall and painted deep red, so it strikes a commanding presence on the quiet flow of Matheson's Brook. It is typical of nineteenth-century gristmills, with a barrier dam directing the waters of the gentle brook into a flume and onto a waterwheel. This simply designed mill has been grinding wheat, oats, and buckwheat for over one hundred years. Sometimes the kiln is toasting oats inside and the aroma drifts out on the breeze.

There was likely only a small section of shallow rapids here before some industrious Scottish immigrants decided to build the dam. On first sight, the larger Waughs River, just a few kilometres to the west, must have seemed a more logical place to establish a mill. There is even a place called "The Falls" on the Waugh. The early millers, however, decided Matheson's Brook was a better mill site, most likely because this smaller stream is not subject to the spring rush and autumn droughts, as the Waugh River is.

Matheson's Brook emerges from a dark valley just above the mill. Old hardwoods lean over the head pond and small wetland creatures scurry along the bank. A set of stairs descends from the parking lot level to the top of the dam, where a walkway leads to the entrance of the mill itself. The tableau pleads with visitors to take a photo.

The brook does have its moments of fury. After a particularly rainy spring, or an occasional summer storm, the rush of water is so great that most of it runs directly over the dam. A scene reminiscent of a time long past is created as the sun shines down on the falls and the wheel turns wildly next to the old red building.

The sound of the splashing water, as it rotates the wheel, spinning the shafts and turning the old millstones, is the music of pioneer Nova Scotia. Perhaps it is no orchestral melody, but at one time this was the harmony of commerce, celebrating the end of an all-too-short growing season and a rare opportunity for a cash return. Sights and sounds like these have all but disappeared today, except for the few places where the importance of falling water is celebrated.

Cuties Hollow

Unfortunately, the origin of the name given to this falls is not recorded anywhere in the popular literature of Nova Scotia. It is a shame that nobody knows what lovely lass might have been the inspiration.

Of course, this is an old province and many generations of settlers have come and gone from these lands, obscuring all but the very notable references, or the very royal. Still, the falls are cute although showing the weight of eons of time. The broad bowl through which the water now flows shows countless stress fractures, and tons of rock at the base give evidence to the fact that the face is slowly wearing away.

The falls are hidden in the hills north of the Trans-Canada Highway at Marshy Hope, where there is a small collection of hunting camps. Summer residents have marked the two-kilometre path as it follows an original pioneer cart track. The path is well used, but still bursting with local flora and fauna until it drops into a steep and dangerous gorge. While it does receive some minimum maintenance from the local nature club, it is also damp and rutted. Most of the time the trail is given over to weekend adventurers on ATVs, who take a more mechanical pleasure from this rugged land.

While the falls can be seen through the understorey of foliage from points along the path, the final twenty-storey drop into the gorge itself is really the only place to enjoy the cascade. Be warned, though, the descent is not for the faint of heart or muscle. It is steep, and the terrain is very loose.

Whatever the assault on the surrounding lands and whatever the future may bring, there is a timelessness of nature at this site. The events of the past are faint memories, the future is yet to be told, but Cuties Hollow stands as it has through it all—with majesty.

Myles Doyle Falls

Myles Doyle Falls is a peaceful site. It is dark and maybe even a little eerie, living continuously in the shadow of a heavy overstorey of old softwoods. Still, many visitors find it beautiful.

A winding dirt lane leads off the Trans-Canada Highway at Melford, and from there, the journey in is short. The dirt road is met by a well-worn footpath, which descends into the wooded hollow off to the right where the falls are located. Some thoughtful local residents have installed a picnic table but left the site dressed in its natural beauty.

The wet rock face has been carved into interesting shapes by the water and if you take the time, the shapes change as the water flushes over them and the shadows grow longer. The cascade is not very full as the stream drains only a portion of a small mountain called "The Big Ridge." Myles Doyle Falls is actually one of the quietest waterfalls in Nova Scotia. Seeming to emerge from a spout in the upper rocks, the water makes a pleasant trickling sound, so that it adds to the peace of the site, blending in with the other sounds of the forest, augmenting them rather than overwhelming them. Myles Doyle Falls is a most meditative spot.

Pipers Glen

Like so many places in Cape Breton, this lovely site near Scotsdale is referred to by many local names. With "Pipers Glen" being such a common name in Scotland, and in Canada as well, some call this site Egypt Falls, although it is not located on the nearby Egypt River. The waterfall is actually on Matheson Glen Brook, where a fault line separates the largely siltstone and sandstone formations. Like the whole of the Upper Margaree Valley, the

waterfall is one of the prettiest natural sanctuaries on Cape Breton Island, regardless of what it is called.

The meandering trail leads across rolling hills for most of the short journey in, winding between young hardwoods with a thick understorey of new saplings and plenty of wildflowers. At the lip of the gorge, a rope is secured to the trees, placed to assist with both the descent and the return from the base of the falls. In autumn, the whole site is aflame with a brilliant display of leafy colour. When the falls are flush with water, in spring or after a good rainfall, the broad rock face fills with a sheet of whitewater.

Even in times of reduced flow, the leafy canopy, the pesky mosquitoes, and the rising mist at the base of the gorge can still evoke visions of a lonely piper, striding along the trail and serenading the sun as it slowly leaves the gorge in the twilight.

Uisge Bahn

Uisge Bahn (yoosh-ghi ban), also called Easach Ban, was the name given to this delightful site by early Gaelic settlers. Roughly translated, it means "Whiskey Falls," but the pioneers knew their water, and their whiskey, a whole lot better than that. Locals will tell you that what was really meant was that the falls offer the water of life, flowing endlessly and having the ability to serve countless future generations to this rocky land. They had the same feelings about their whiskey, too.

With its fetching name, its location on Falls Brook just a few kilometres north of Baddeck, and the splendidly moody gorge that surrounds it, this site has become a tourist mecca. Provincial officials have recognized this and promote the waterfall as one of the best ways to enjoy a hands-on visit to Cape Breton. The province cares well for the site, providing the needed trail amenities and protection for the surrounding natural habitat, ensuring that the abundant wildlife the water supports will endure as long as the falls themselves.

The two-kilometre trail to the site is quite suitable for most visitors. There are a few small hills but no steep slopes, and several rest stops are provided. Attractive footbridges have been located at a number of stream crossings, adding to the enjoyment of this wilderness adventure. A sudden narrowing of the valley and a floating mist forewarn of the final few steps to the falls. The roar of the five-storey cascade as it drops into the pool below almost drowns out conversation. Most hikers are tired and perspiring at this point and the idea of a quick dip in the dark water comes to mind. The water is too cold for swimming, however, even in summer, so most visitors settle for a drink. Somehow just one slurp from this mountain oasis seems to provide an immediate energy boost.

It is a beautiful site, one that affords Nova Scotia bragging rights for having such a dramatic waterfall. Hikers who have completed the trip brag as well, about having tasted the magical "waters of life."

North River Falls

Cape Breton

North River Falls in Cape Breton, (facing page), stands like a reigning monarch. It is the highest waterfall in the province, and perhaps the most statuesque. It was this stature that convinced officials to create the North River Wilderness Area, protecting the upper reaches of the river, including the falls, along with the neighbouring backcountry areas and the Little Falls (below). Knowing that this attractive enclave will someday be extremely popular as a wilderness hiking destination, provincial officials moved in advance to protect the still-pristine environment from development. In an attempt to reduce the impact of more and more hikers, they established a trail, but the simple amenities most visitors might enjoy on a trek into this site are few and far between.

While the arduous, nine-kilometre walk to the falls discourages many, gazing upon this hidden treasure is the reward for those who do make the journey. Because the gorge is broad and sunlit, a variety of photo opportunities is possible. The trail leads right to the base of the falls, so there is no need to scramble down a loose rock wall to get the best view. The rock formations offer many places to sit for a picnic and the cool waterfall pool provides a natural

spa for the hot and tired hiker. There is a steep path to the top of the gorge, many hundreds of metres up, but the view it provides seems less awesome than the one from the base. Up there the roar of crashing water is lost in the wind, no spray covers your face, and the connection with one of Cape Breton's natural wonders seems too faint.

Great Falls

There are falls in Cape Breton that are easy to walk to and others that are difficult, but Great Falls is simply impossible to access on foot. A canoe is almost mandatory for this trip, making visiting this site one of the more memorable waterfall outings. That having been said, the journey is still difficult

Indian Brook is a small village not more than ten to twelve kilometres up the Cabot Trail from where the Englishtown ferry docks. The highway actually crosses the brook a short distance before the community, and at that point is the most likely place to launch a canoe for the trip up river.

The voyage includes about two kilometres of paddling up a shallow stream and several portages over gravel bars that cross the path. The falls finally appear around one last craggy outcrop just when it seems impossible to lift the canoe any further.

Great Falls is the first of several cascades on this long river and certainly one of the most impressive in the province. Its name comes not from its great height, as the drop is less than ten metres, but for the grandeur of the wide waterfall bowl that fills this natural stage. When the summer sun shines into this classic amphitheatre, the water glistens as it tumbles down into the large pool below.

On the trip back, watch the western shore for a hidden waterfall. It is actually higher than Great Falls, and only a few metres in from the shore of the brook. Shrouded by the thick young hardwoods, and perched on loose rocks, it is hard to get a great view of these bonus falls, but the aura of this rough and misty site is another image that will be hard to forget.

Corney Brook Falls

Cape Breton Highlands National Park is blessed with the right combination of a broad, marshy upland plateau, and a number of streams that drain the area before they drop dramatically to the ocean. Park planners have been generous with their trail development projects here and several of the park's twenty-seven advertised routes follow the rivers, offering easy access to waterfalls sites.

The well-marked trail into Corney Brook winds along the brook through a deep valley and showcases its geology, the extremely varied foliage, and the wildlife that inhabits it. The trail leads through a variety of rock outcroppings, making the journey a chance to come face-to-face with many of the rock types displayed at the Cape Breton Highlands National Park geology exhibit in Cheticamp. Formations with odd-sounding names like schist and gneiss become recognizable as the path follows the grey rock cliffs.

A box canyon at the end of the trail provides the highlight of the route. Here, the water of Corney Brook Falls tumbles fifteen metres over the cliff, sometimes in one plume, sometimes

 separated by the rocks into two or more streams. The surrounding topography offers some natural spots to pause and take in the view, creatively framing the waterfall like a backdrop.

MacIntosh Brook Falls

At MacIntosh Brook, it is the nature trail to the falls that really makes this a memorable site. Starting from a well-signed picnic area north of Cheticamp, the walk is a groomed and popular attraction in this national park. There are actually two fairly level trails following the stream here, one on each of the banks and both resplendent with a superb variety of boreal flora and fauna. Information on all the plant and animal species is readily available at park interpretative centres in Cheticamp and Ingonish.

Once at the falls, there are lots of rock outcroppings and fallen trees, giving the picturesque, if somewhat sideways, waterfall a wilderness aura. The site is fairly flat, however, so it is easy to explore all around and even up the falls.

There are also a few smaller falls upstream through the steeper parts of the gorge, but none has a more attractive wading pool than the main site. While most waterfalls are perched inside craggy rock gorges, children will enjoy being able to explore these falls—even getting close to the pool—without too much worry from parents that they will get their shoes wet "by mistake." On the way back from the falls, be sure to check one of the wildlife guidebooks available at the park interpretative centre for fascinating information on the little creatures that call MacIntosh Brook their home.

Mary Ann Falls

As the glaciers receded, scouring the bedrock and carving out a rough channel in the granite and gneiss—a layered rock made up of mica, feldspar, and quartz—the gorge that holds Mary Ann Falls was left behind. It is rugged but still beautiful and very accessible, with a well-maintained road leading right to the top of the gorge. The park management has also provided plenty of parking, washrooms, and viewing platforms. With access to this pretty site being so easy, it is always fairly crowded and everyone seems to enjoy the view. The more daring visitors jump off the rocks, some from great heights.

Each season there are many international visitors who put Mary Ann Falls on their itinerary. It is certainly not a match for Niagara Falls, but it is a lovely and wide cascade that offers great photo opportunities for travellers. It is a little like Niagara Falls in another way: It claims to be the top spot in Nova Scotia for wedding proposals.

In the early morning, before human visitors arrive, moose are often seen here, munching

away on the bushes beside the road. For the most part, moose avoid the tourist season here, but occasionally a foreign tourist is surprised by one. Niagara Falls can't offer that!

Island View Falls

Visiting these falls in Cape Breton is a great outing for the family. The kids will appreciate the short drive down from Sydney to the East Bay shores of the Bras d'Or Lakes. The walk into the site is only about one kilometre, taking less than thirty minutes. Best of all, the only way in is up the stream bed itself, wading in sometimes knee-deep water, so children of all ages will have fun getting wet. Just before the last turn in the stream, the terrain becomes a little more difficult as the rocks get larger. Then the familiar low roar of a nearby waterfall reaches your ears and the rocks seem to get smaller again.

The falls tumble diagonally, so they appear much higher than they actually are. For the most part, they face the southeast, so if there is any sun at all, it will be sparkling off the many ledges, welcoming visitors to this open and airy waterfall canyon. While getting wet is not a problem, getting hungry might be, as this site really requires an extended stay; there is just so much interesting scenery to explore. Be sure to pack a hearty picnic lunch, and dry socks for the drive home.

Carding Mill Falls

Nova Scotia is dotted with hundreds of once-productive mill sites. This particular site is just upstream from the cable ferry dock on the eastern side of Country Harbour. A canoe is needed to travel the one kilometre to a hidden cove just north of the ferry ramp, as there is no access by land. Once in the cove behind Mount Misery, the waterfall is just a short walk along a well-trodden woodland trail next to the stream. The actual waterfall is on Carding Mill Brook, a long and winding stream that is part of the drainage of Big Plains, a huge inland bog.

In spite of its natural beauty and the obvious attraction it held for pioneer settlers as a mill site, it's hard to imagine that there ever was a permanent establishment at this site. True, Country Harbour is a natural haven from the turbulent Atlantic Ocean, and it has always provided abundant fish harvests, but it is a mystery why early immigrants, with little to work with, chose to invest such effort on this rocky shore, so far from other communities. There it remains, however, after all the intervening generations: a stone foundation of the carding mill, right where a diversion flume would have directed the water flow from its original course onto the water wheel.

With the passing of time, nature has done its best to reclaim what the early settlers created. Blueberry and bunchberry vines overwhelm those hand-placed stones, and the young softwoods of a new forest now grow up inside the walls.

The flow of the stream has returned to its original path as well, ignoring the spot where it was once redirected into the flume. Rich, tawny water again descends the ten-metre gorge in a crooked rush, spraying a fine mist as it bounces off the many small ledges that create a natural spa for plant life. The area is actually quite mossy and the soil is rich underfoot. Maybe it was that this high soil quality, combined with the value of the water power, which encouraged the settlement here. Or maybe it was just the experience of reaching the rugged shore by small boat, hiking through the pleasant forest, and letting the misty waterfall plume bathe the senses.

Sherbrooke Village Mill Falls

Regardless of its location, falling water has been important to Nova Scotians for generations and no more important than its use at mill sites. Whether for generating hydroelectricity, grinding grain, or sawing the lumber needed for new homes, water power helped build Nova Scotia. That is evident in Sherbrooke, where falling water at a restored sawmill cut much of the lumber used in the modern reconstruction of the popular pioneer village.

There is something about watching a wheel spin that captivates the human spirit. In a village like Sherbrooke, where perhaps the busy times have all passed, it's nice to take a few moments to watch water and wheel in motion together.

Unlike most sawmill sites, there never was a waterfall here originally. Early engineers thought it would work best if they diverted water from a nearby lake by digging an eight-hundred-and-fifty-metre canal and establishing a waterfall. A holding pond was then created with a ten-metre drop, powering the big saw blades.

Natural or not, the mill was an immediate success and pivotal to the creation of the nearby town. Several generations later, a new mill was constructed on the site, and sawed the lumber needed for the major restoration of Sherbrooke Village. Now that the project is complete, the mill's productive days are done, but the site is still a welcome rest stop on the journey along the Eastern Shore.

Liscomb Falls

The waters of the Liscomb River are famous for many things, not the least of which is the lovely dark ale colour noticed by so many people as they drive along the Eastern Shore highway. Nature has been very kind to this area, and particularly to Liscomb, for the splendid colours of the woods and waters, and of the shore and sky, attract many visitors. People come in the spring to experience the long-awaited return of the lush green foliage and return in the fall to bathe in the splendour of that same leafy canopy as it turns to red and brilliant yellow. The magic of a tawny waterfall just adds to the enjoyment of the whole area.

The nearby Liscombe Lodge Resort offers a beautiful tourist destination, with cabins, wilderness trails, boat rentals, and other attractions that have opened up the area to summer visitors. In winter, the temperatures rarely drop low enough for the river to become completely frozen over, allowing the brown water to sweep over the grey rock ledges and to flood the ice clinging to the shores. Locals enjoy the river at this time of year, as the rocks are often clear of snow and rambling over the ledges is a pleasant way to spend an afternoon. The falls themselves are a series of broad quartzite ledges and small cascades, as opposed to one long waterfall. There is an ongoing debate about how high a site should be before it can actually be called a "waterfall." Liscomb Falls is so well known, however, that most people

refer to it as a waterfall, even though it is a very small drop.

The Liscomb River is a very popular river. Travellers come from all over the Maritimes to hike, fish, and canoe the waterway. Most will stay below the falls for their canoeing, but there are those who try their luck at running the falls from the cabins above. It rarely ends happily. Perhaps it was at Liscomb that the popular definition of a waterfall was first described: any descent that cannot be successfully negotiated by canoe.

West River Falls

One of the very first inlets on the Eastern Shore to be explored by the early Europeans was Sheet Harbour. Taking its name from the great white rock that marks its entrance, this safe anchorage was conveniently close to the richest fishing grounds the Portuguese and Spanish fishermen had ever seen. It also provided teeming runs of Atlantic salmon and abundant fresh water from the West and East Rivers of Sheet Harbour. When the visiting fishermen decided to build permanent colonies here, they recognized the junction of these two streams as the best site for their new community.

To the wave of settlers who followed soon after the explorers, the West River offered other important advantages: multiple waterfalls and free mill power. And so it was that Sheet Harbour became known as a mill town for almost two hundred years. By the 1960s, however, pulp and lumber mills were no longer earning a return on the huge investment they required.

To the concern of town officials, the mill at Sheet Harbour was closed and almost completely removed from the site.

To the absolute delight of the town's residents, however, the stunning waterfall site that was once so overshadowed by the mill shone brilliantly. Golden-coloured water could again be seen as it cascaded over the many steps and ledges just below the Highway 7 bridge. Where people once averted their glance from an industrial eyesore, they now marvelled at how attractive their river actually was.

Tourist operators began actively promoting the site as a "must see" on the Eastern Shore. An information bureau was established next to the river, along with a new walking trail and a footbridge that offers the best vantage points for pictures of the lovely falls. One of the first sites on the coast to be valued by pioneer visitors became one of the most recent sites to be rediscovered by their descendants.

If the Atlantic salmon could only rebound to the point where they would again be seen jumping from ledge to ledge up these splendid falls, the circle would be complete.

Unnamed Falls

Once a storied Atlantic salmon river, the Musquodoboit River's spawning run has been reduced to very few, protected fish. As it meanders down to the Eastern Shore, it is still a destination for hundreds of nature lovers, however, and remains one of the most peaceful places to spend an afternoon. Only a few small rapids break up the river's gentle flow over the sixty kilometres it travels from its headwaters to the sea. Standing in sharp contrast to the mostly peaceful river is at least one huge waterfall, hidden near the source of the river's South Branch. There, not far from the pioneer settlement of Dean, the water surges over twenty metres of rock ledge into a very forbidding gorge.

The falls were likely discovered by early timber barons seeking old-growth stands of valuable wood to harvest and ship back to England. Many of the forest workers and their families also settled the land, opened up the new resources, and developed the emerging

economy. The area near the falls, though, save for a small amount of gypsum mining, has remained undeveloped and underpopulated and has been quickly reclaimed by nature. Thick mosses and fungi cover the old stumps that remain. Blueberry and raspberry bushes overwhelm any signs of industrial activity and what timber harvesting that does occur in the area is now restricted from coming too close to the water's edge.

Wildlife abounds here. Plants like choke cherry and sarsaparilla, as well as hawks, hares, and even eels, all share the quiet bounty of the site. Actually, the tiny eels that can be seen at these falls are at the elver stage of their life cycle, which sees them migrate inland from the ocean all the way up to these falls and then make a supreme effort to climb the ancient schist and slate face to their future home in Cox Flowage, at the river's headwaters. How the tiny elvers can overcome such impediments to migration remains a wonder of life.

Many recreational anglers now hope that the salmon and trout will also be able to overcome the difficulties that have reduced their numbers and return, like the eels, to the famous Musquodoboit River.

New Brunswick

• Amherst

Pugwash

Cape Chignecto •   ㉕   ㉔

                                   • Parrsboro
                              ㉓ ㉒ ㉑
                                        ⑳ ⑲ ⑱
                         ⑦   ⑰

                                 Wolfville •
   ⑥   ⑧   Tru
• Digby •   • Bridgetown
⑤   Windsor •
                                   ⑨   ① ⑪
   ④
                                              ⑩
          ③
Nova Scotia   Mahone Bay •   Halifax • • Dartmouth
                           Lunenburg •
• Yarmouth

              Liverpool •
      • Shelburne

① Dawson Brook Falls	⑨ Millet Falls
② Indian Falls (LaHave River)	⑩ Sleepy Cove Falls
③ Mill Falls	⑪ St. Croix Falls
④ Indian Falls (Meteghan River)	⑫ Butchers Falls
⑤ Lake Brook Falls	⑬ Upper Burnside Falls
⑥ Delaps Cove Falls	⑭ Fall Brook Falls
⑦ Baxters Harbour Falls	⑮ Victoria Park Falls
⑧ Moores Falls	⑯ Annandale Falls
	⑰ Wentworth Valley Falls
	⑱ Londonderry Falls

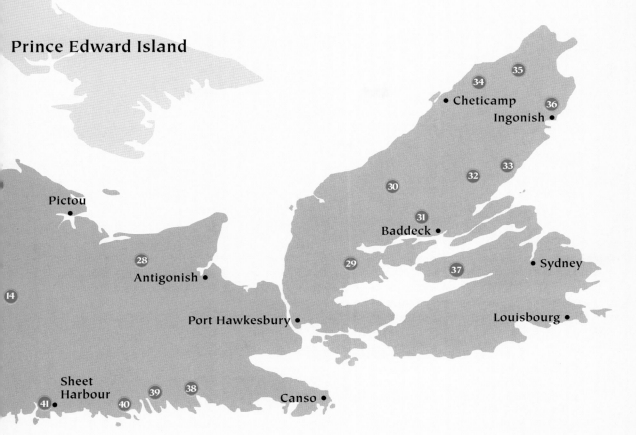

Prince Edward Island

Cheticamp •

Ingonish •

Pictou •

Baddeck •

• Sydney

Antigonish •

Port Hawkesbury •

Louisbourg •

Sheet
Harbour

Canso •

⑲ Economy Falls	㉛ Uisge Bahn (or Easach Ban)
⑳ North River Falls (Cobequid Range)	㉜ North River Falls (Cape Breton)
㉑ Harrington Falls	㉝ Great Falls
㉒ Moose River Falls	㉞ Corney Brook Falls
㉓ Hidden Falls	㉟ MacIntosh Brook Falls
㉔ Ripley Falls	㊱ Mary Ann Falls
㉕ Wards Falls	㊲ Island View Falls
㉖ Drysdale Falls	㊳ Carding Mill Falls
㉗ Balmoral Mills	㊴ Sherbrooke Village Mill Falls
㉘ Cuties Hollow	㊵ Liscomb Falls
㉙ Myles Doyle Falls	㊶ West River Falls
㉚ Pipers Glen	㊷ Unnamed Falls

Directions Index

Numbers in circles correspond to map

16 **Annandale Falls, page 30**

Only five kilometres west of the Wentworth Valley, on Route 246, an unmarked wood road leads south up into the Cobequid Mountains. Just before a fork in that road, and less than a kilometre in, there is a wide area for parking. A rugged trail on the right leads to the top of the falls. There is no access to the base of the gorge from here.

27 **Balmoral Mills, page 53**

Balmoral Mills Provincial Park is on Route 256, just three kilometres east of the intersection with Route 311. It is well-signed with a large parking lot at the top of the path leading to the mill. The falls are beside the mill. A stairway down to the riverbed at the bottom of the cascade provides a unique vantage point if there is not too much water coming over the dam.

7 **Baxters Harbour Falls, page 13**

Baxters Harbour is on a little-known road along the Bay of Fundy shore, north of Kentville. Take Route 359 towards Halls Harbour for about twelve kilometres. Turn right towards West Glenmont for about five kilometres and then left towards Baxters Harbour for another eight kilometres. These falls can be seen from the community's fishing wharf, right down on the beach.

12 **Butchers Falls, page 22**

The gravel road between Upper Musquodoboit and Upper Stewiacke crosses the boundary between the Halifax Regional Municipality and Colchester County. On the Colchester side of that line, the road climbs out of the Musquoboboit Valley, passes through some blueberry fields, and descends into the Stewiacke River watershed. The Butchers' abandoned homestead is on the right, coming down the hill. It marks the trailhead to the falls. The path is on the opposite side of the road from the old home, but spruce trees obscure it. Walk down the road and listen for the falls. They are only one hundred metres in.

38 **Carding Mill Falls, page 74**

Just past Sherbrooke, on Highway 7, take the right-hand turn onto Highway 211 and follow the signs for the Country Harbour ferry, about thirty kilometres away. Park in the lot at the ferry terminal and launch a canoe or dory right where the ferry lands. It is an easy paddle northward for a kilometre, through the many buoys of a mussel farm and around the headland of Mount Misery. Tucked in the pleasant cove behind the headland is a rocky beach and the outflow of Carding Mill Brook. The mill site and falls are a ten-minute walk up the stream.

34 **Corney Brook Falls, page 66**

Just twelve kilometres into the Cape Breton Highlands National Park from the Cheticamp side, Corney Brook runs under the Cabot Trail and into the Gulf of St. Lawrence. There is a well-signed trail up to the falls that is maintained by park staff. The journey is four kilometres each way.

28 **Cuties Hollow, page 54**

From a signed intersection on the Trans-Canada Highway at Marshy Hope, a dirt road leads north for about six-and-a-half kilometres. At a clearing dotted with a few hunters' cabins, a small sign points out the trail to the falls. The James River gorge is two kilometres farther in, on a rutted track, dotted with swamps and washouts, but the way is level until the top of the gorge is reached. The falls can be seen from the top, and a rope may be tied to the trees, marking the way down, but the access to the falls is extremely steep and there is no place to rest, or even to stand comfortably, at the base.

1 **Dawson Brook Falls, page 1**
Take Exit 4 off Highway 101 and follow the side road south through Hartville and Ellershouse. From there, cross the bridge to the left and follow the new gravel road, which parallels the highway for three kilometres back towards Halifax. At that point, there is another dirt road leading off to the right that passes through a logging area. Just 250 metres along is a wide spot where you can park your car and follow the unmarked trail north into a wonderful stand of white pine trees. The falls are just a few hundred metres in, on the left. You will hear them before you see them.

6 **Delaps Cove Falls, page 10**
Follow Highway 1 to the tidal power dam and causeway just outside of Annapolis Royal. There is a well-signed intersection pointing the way to the historic Habitation Port Royal. Just a few hundred metres before the fortress, turn right towards Delaps Cove and then left when you reach the road along the Bay of Fundy shore. Continue through the tiny hamlet and look for a dirt road off to the left just before a campground. Follow this hilly track for two kilometres to a parking spot and small trailhead. There are pit toilets here and an interpretive sign. The trail into the falls is a circular loop of just under two kilometres in total, and you can follow it in either direction.

26 **Drysdale Falls, page 50**
These falls are located on Route 256, about four kilometres west of the intersection with Route 311, and are well-marked on most maps. They are on private land, however, and permission must be obtained from the landowner before accessing the short trail up Bailey's Brook to the top of the falls.

19 **Economy Falls, page 37**
The turnoff for Economy Falls is about twelve kilometres west of Bass River on Route 2. Turn right and head up into the hills for seven kilometres, following the signs for the falls. There is a a pit toilet and a parking lot with a nice view of the valley. The trail to the falls starts there and meanders for another kilometre until it meets the long, long staircase to the base of the falls.

14 **Fall Brook Falls, page 26**
Following Route 289 westward, drive one kilometre past the Pictou–Colchester County line. A path leads off to the south at that point. This old cart track passes by a hunter's cabin and through some pioneer farmland. Less than two kilometres along, the path meets Fall Brook and the falls are just downstream.

33 **Great Falls, page 65**
To access these falls, you must park next to the bridge where the Cabot Trail crosses Indian Brook and launch your canoe from the gravel bank on the south side. The trip upstream requires paddling across four deep pools and dragging the boat up over many rocks and several gravel bars for about three kilometres. When you cannot lift the canoe up over any more rocky ledges, tie it to the alder bushes at the edge of the water and walk the final few hundred metres to the falls.

21 **Harrington Falls, page 41**
Access to Harrington Falls is up the Lynn Road, a well-marked right-hand turn off Route 2. Follow this road north for approximately four-and-a-half kilometres, and then keep a sharp eye out for the trailhead. Actually, it is just a small clearing on the left side of the road, marked by a piece of flagging tape and some litter. The trail wanders off for about twenty minutes until the top of the gorge is reached, where the sound of the falls might be heard. A very difficult track leads down into the gorge, one that seems much steeper on the climb back out.

23 **Hidden Falls, page 45**
Hidden Falls is not far from a field right next to the north side of Route 2, about seven kilometres east of Parrsboro. There was a homestead on this land until a few years ago and remnants of its foundation may still be seen. Now the land is used by a few paragliders and they sometimes leave their windsock mounted on a pole there. The trail leads a few hundred metres up into the woods from the back of the field. It is unmarked and overgrown but short and safe for most walkers.

2 Indian Falls (LaHave River), page 2

Turn inland (north) on Exit 11 from Highway 103 and follow Route 324. About two kilometres past Upper New Cornwall, take the eastern fork of the intersection, and drive another five kilometres. There is a new gravel access road on the left-hand side that leads the one kilometre into the parking lot. The falls are just a few steps farther.

4 Indian Falls (Meteghan River), page 6

Indian Falls can be seen from the old steel-truss bridge on the road from Meteghan River to St. Benoni. There is really no place to park and enjoy the view, other than the side of this narrow roadway. There is no trail to the falls.

37 Island View Falls, page 73

Following Highway 216 south from Sydney River, these falls are just a few kilometres east of the Eskasoni Reserve. There is a small white bridge where MacIntosh Brook runs under the road, and a few parking spots next to that. The falls are one kilometre upstream, but the only way in is up the shallow brook.

5 Lake Brook Falls, page 9

Follow Route 217 down Digby Neck to the village of Sandy Cove. Turn left toward the fishing wharf, but at the T-intersection, continue to the left again as the road narrows into a rutted track. In a few minutes, a fine old white home appears on the left, with an area to park on the right. If the residents are at home, ask their permission to cross their land. The path is obscure from here but it basically follows the stream to the top of the falls. Getting down to the base of the cascade is almost impossible.

40 Liscomb Falls, page 78

Highway 7 crosses the Liscomb River pretty much at the base of these falls. A parking lot has been established on the south side, just across the bridge, so visitors can get out of their cars and return on foot to the grassy banks right at the falls.

18 Londonderry Falls, page 34

Londonderry is west of Highway 4, just before the highway climbs Folly Mountain and then descends into the Wentworth Valley. From a well-signed intersection, drive five kilometres west. Proceed through the old townsite, and cross the bridge over Rockland Brook. Turn right and follow the dirt road north. There is a right-hand turn onto the road that leads to "Manager's Park" and the parking area at the top of the falls.

35 MacIntosh Brook Falls, page 69

Some forty-five kilometres into the Cape Breton Highlands National Park from the Cheticamp side, and almost at the end of the long climb up that part of MacKenzie Mountain, is the well-signed rest area at MacIntosh Brook. The trail leaves from the parking area on the right-hand side of the Cabot Trail. It is fairly flat and only 1.4 kilometres each way.

36 Mary Ann Falls, page 70

Visitors can get right up to Mary Ann Falls by car. The access road is near Broad Cove, about thirty kilometres up the Cabot Trail from the Ingonish entrance to Cape Breton Highlands National Park. It is a seven-kilometre drive to the parking lot, where park staff have prepared several look-off points.

3 Mill Falls, page 5

These falls are located in Kejimkujik National Park, just behind the park's visitor services building. To get to the park from Halifax, follow Highway 103 towards Liverpool, and take Exit 19 north for about seventy kilometres. Once at the main parking lot, either follow the pretty nature trail a few hundred metres to the falls, or drive a little farther to the picnic shelter and park there. The falls are directly behind the shelter.

9 Millet Falls, page 17

Halfway between Windsor and Chester on Highway 114 is the community of Vaughan. About four kilometres north of Vaughan, turn west in the direction of New Ross and drive less than two kilometres to find the private road that accesses the cottages on the western shores of Falls Lake. At the end of this pleasant drive is a short walk to the base of the falls.

8 Moores Falls, page 14

Moores Brook flows under Highway 101 just one kilometre west of Exit 13. The falls are on the right-hand side when travelling east towards Halifax and are visible from that side of the highway. There is even a rough trail from there down to the base of the falls but, unfortunately, there is very little room to pull over.

22 Moose River Falls, page 42

These falls are unmarked, but the adventurous hikers who do visit them each year have left a few clues as to their location. There is an old dirt road leading north into the hills from Route 2, about twelve kilometres east of Parrsboro. It starts at a point between the two bridges west of the community of Moose River. Following that road for about two kilometres takes you up near some blueberry fields and an old tree on the left, with winch-cable marks on its trunk. That is about the only marker for the short and rough trail down into the gorge. Climbing into and out of the gorge is made very hazardous by all the loose rock and a perpendicular cliff face.

29 Myles Doyle Falls, page 57

Follow the Trans-Canada Highway east from the Canso causeway for thirty-five kilometres. The road to River Denys Mountain turns off to the left at that point and the falls are one kilometre up that road. There is no place to park, but you can pull your car to the side of the road. A small sign may be nailed to a tree on the right-hand side, marking a steep but short trail down into the falls.

32 North River Falls (Cape Breton), page 62

The trail begins at a well-maintained picnic park in the pioneer settlement of Oregon, a few kilometres north of North River Bridge on the Cabot Trail. There is an information kiosk in the park, as well as signs leading to both the left and Little Falls, and to the right for the nine-kilometre trail to the main falls. The trail is well-marked and fairly flat, but there are a lot of steep slopes and slippery rock faces along the route to the falls.

20 North River Falls (Cobequid Range), page 38

Along Route 2, some twenty-six kilometres west of Bass River, the Little York Road turns right, up into the hills. Follow that dirt road for three kilometres, and just before a modern-looking cedar home, there is a narrow lane grown over in alder bushes. Ask for the permission of the landowner there to follow the lane about a kilometre to a clearing where cars can be parked. From there it is an easy walk, following the well-worn path, to the top of the gorge. Descending into the gorge is a challenge, however, and can only be done safely by clinging hand-over-hand to the rope left tied to the trees.

30 Pipers Glen, page 58

Follow Highway 395 north along Lake Ainslie. Approximately three kilometres past the community of Scotsville, a sign for Pipers Glen and Egypt Brook should mark the right turn onto a dirt road. About two kilometres up that road is a bridge marking another right turn onto a wood road. After one more kilometre, a sign on the right may mark the trailhead. The wooded path is then less than a kilometre walk, but the last section includes a straight drop down into the gorge—a very difficult descent.

24 Ripley Falls, page 46

Just a few kilometres north of Parrsboro is a collection of century-old homes called Lakelands, overlooking Jeffers Lake. Atop the rise on the eastern side of the water, where Jeffers Brook crosses under the road and runs into the lake, is a large white house owned by the Ripleys. A path leads back up along that brook behind their home for a hundred metres, to the base of the falls. It is always polite to ask for permission to cross private land.

11 St. Croix Falls, page 21

These falls have been created by the power station at St. Croix on Highway 1, just a dozen or so kilometres east of Windsor. They tumble over a dam right at the side of the roadway.

39 Sherbrooke Village Mill Falls, page 77

Following the signs to historic Sherbrooke Village, it is easy to locate the mill site on the north side of town. There the stream falls over the dam right beside the road, and a parking lot offers a good vantage point.

10 Sleepy Cove Falls, page 18

Follow the Waverley Road (Route 2) north from Dartmouth to Wellington. Turn west onto the old King Road, crossing the railway tracks and following it past numerous lakefront lots to its end, almost seven kilometres later. From there, the brook and its falls are a short walk along a natural path.

31 Uisge Bahn (Easach Ban), page 61

From Exit 9 on the Trans-Canada Highway near Baddeck, follow the signs for Forks Baddeck. It is about fourteen kilometres from the exit. A provincial park has grown up around the falls, including a parking lot, signposts, and information with directions from the trailhead to the falls. The well-maintained trail is less than two kilometres long and offers benches, direction indicators, and amenities.

42 Unnamed Falls, page 82

The community of Upper Musquodoboit is on Route 336, near the boundary line between Halifax Regional Municipality and Colchester County. Just eleven kilometres north of Upper Musquodoboit there is a gravel road leading east into an area of commercial forestry operations. After one kilometre, look for a small clearing on the right and an obscure path through the new growth. It leads to the top of the falls, about four hundred metres to the east.

13 Upper Burnside Falls, page 25

Take Route 289 up the Stewiacke River Valley to Stewiacke Cross Roads. This small hamlet marks a junction with the dirt road that crosses the backcountry all the way to the Trans-Canada Highway at Kemptown. Some twelve kilometres up that road, and on the right-hand side, the residents of Upper Burnside have created a small picnic park. There is a parking lot, a flagpole, and a long stairway leading down to the base of the falls.

15 Victoria Park Falls, page 29

In the town of Truro, follow Prince Street east until it meets Brunswick Street. Not far from there is the entrance to Victoria Park. The nature trails to the falls are just past the swimming pool and are well-marked.

25 Wards Falls, page 49

The community of Wharton is eight kilometres west of Parrsboro, on Highway 209. Take a right-hand turn at the sign for Wards Falls and follow the road to a parking area, where the trail to the falls begins. The residents here are proud to have such an attraction for visitors and try to maintain several signs and the three-and-a-half kilometre trail each year.

17 Wentworth Valley Falls, page 33

Follow the old Highway 4 north from Truro and Folly Lake. Just two kilometres past the large gravel operation in Folly Lake is a dirt track off the western side of the road. It is marked by a steel gatepost but is generally open and cars can access the site. The base of the falls is a pleasant two-hundred-metre walk from there.

41 West River Falls, page 81

Seen from the Highway 7 bridge over the West River, there is perhaps a better view from the parking lot just past the bridge on the right side. Follow the short nature trail down the eastern side of the river to a long footbridge seemingly made for photographers.